# WATER'S WAY

## Life Along the Chesapeake

For Barbara, Hilary, and Alison
*DWH*

*(Pages 2-3) Great blue heron, Cat Point Creek, Rappahannock River.*
*(Pages 4-5) Pocomoke River.*
*(Pages 6-7) Tassels of phragmites grass.*
*(Pages 8-9) Nancy Ann, Backlanding Marsh, Smith Island.*
*(Pages 10-11) Peach Blossom Harbor, Tilghman Island.*

Designed by Gibson Parsons Design
Edited by Carolyn M. Clark
Captions by David W. Harp and Tom Horton
ISBN 1-880216-01-9
Printed in Singapore by Tien Wah Press
5 4 3 2 1     1999 1998 1997 1996 1995 1994 1993 1992

Library of Congress Cataloguing-In-Publication Data
Harp, David W.
Water's way: life along the Chesapeake / photography by David W. Harp: essays by Tom Horton.
p.    cm.
ISBN 1-880216-01-9
1. Natural history—Chesapeake Bay (Md. and Va.) 2. Natural history—Chesapeake Bay (Md. and Va.)—
Pictorial works. 3. Fisheries—Chesapeake Bay (Md. and Va.) 4. Fisheries—Chesapeake Bay (Md. and Va.)—
Pictorial works. 5. Man—Influence on nature—Chesapeake Bay Region (Md. and Va.) 6. Man—Influence on
nature—Chesapeake Bay Region (Md. and Va.)—Pictorial works. 7. Chesapeake Bay (Md. and Va.)—
description and travel. 8. Chesapeake Bay (Md. and Va.)—Description and travel—Views.
I. Horton, Tom, 1945- . II. Title.
QH104.5.C45H37 1992
508.3163'47—dc20                                        91-36706
                                                          CIP

# WATER'S WAY

## Life Along the Chesapeake

Photography by David W. Harp
Essays by Tom Horton
*In Association with the Chesapeake Bay Foundation*

ELLIOTT & CLARK PUBLISHING

*The photograph on this page was literally my backyard on Smith Island; but I never saw it so lovely as portrayed here until a day when one of the heaviest fogs in years wrapped the island in a soft light. It transformed the plain marsh, giving it a textured, painterly, Andrew Wyeth look. Dave Harp was able to catch it.*

*It was luck, and it wasn't. Dave calls it "being there." What he means is that more happens out on the bay at any given time than you could ever imagine. If you only go for the scheduled event, the sure thing, the shots that can be had from dockside, you miss being there when those windows like the* Nancy Ann *shrouded in fog crack open ever so briefly.*

*Sometimes the windows open only slowly. I'm thinking of long, hot hours spent in a plywood blind built 40 feet from nesting herons, and Dave, enveloped in cigar smoke for protection, sharing his four-by-three-foot sauna with hornets and greenheads.*

*The* Nancy Ann *and the herons are among the book's loveliest shots; but* Water's Way *was never conceived as a collection of Dave Harp's prettiest photos. We wanted to illustrate those essential qualities of the Chesapeake that in our long experience make the bay special, and also specially vulnerable to degradation. That tension between how much we have lost of our Chesapeake heritage, and how incredibly much remains, was for both of us during the making of this book sometimes dispiriting, often delightful. Always, it seemed, "being there" was better than anywhere else.*

—Tom Horton

# THE EDGE

I stood in a waterman's run-down shanty where he had shed soft crabs by the creek for 30 years, explaining to him the benefits of modern aquaculture. With the closed-cycle, recirculating saltwater systems the university had developed, he could now produce soft crabs more efficiently and cheaper in a garage in town, I said. As I talked, the August sun dipped low, stoking the marsh out his front door to a tawny incandescence. The bay beyond rimmed the marsh edge with a thin line of pure, molten gold. Blue herons, snowy egrets, and glossy ibis headed back to their roosts, and a flood tide running up the channel beneath the shanty's floor planks carried a delicious cool to the interior. Surf murmured rhythmically on a distant beach. Finally, my friend spoke. That was "right pretty progress alright," he said, some fellow figuring out how you could trade this for garage work.

The edges where land and water meet charm us all, from watermen to watercolorists and beachcombers to duck hunters. They please the eye and feed the soul, and more than any other feature shape our consciousness of the Chesapeake Bay. It is in the coves and marshes and tidal guts of the Chesapeake that we gain first and most frequent acquaintance with the greater bay. In fact, the Chesapeake proper, roughly 200 miles long by up to 20 miles wide, probably is hard to comprehend for most of us. Think of all our river songs and images, and then try to come up with similar ones for bays. "In the public mind, the Bay is often negative space, geographically fuzzy, [lacking] the visual unity to become symbolically powerful," Mary K. Blair once wrote in an essay, "Nature as Symbol." But that all changes wherever the great estuary contacts the lands and wetlands that ring it. In the shallows and indents of the shoreline, the bay gets fined down, lent texture and character that we can see and sample and hear and muck around in.

More than most bodies of water, the bay's edges crinkle and fold, twining intimately with its waters; and more than 40 significant tributary rivers extend and repeat the same process, telegraphing the estuary's tidal pulses and the life of its fishes and birds far into the land.

Imagine that, like Paul Bunyan straightening out a crooked river with one yank, you could grasp

*Scallops of sand, loops and whorls and endless meanders of marsh and tidal creek—the shoreline of the Chesapeake Bay, if it could be unraveled, would easily stretch from coast to coast and back.*

the bay's surrounding lands; take hold down around Accomack and Cape Charles, Virginia; and *snap* it smartly like a whip, cracking wide open the hinge where the eastern and western shores join at the bay's head. Crack it hard enough to unravel every slough and oxbow, every cove and creek for the whole 200-mile length of the bay, up one side and down the other, Susquehanna to James, Piankatank to Pocomoke, Chickahominy to Chester, and Sassafras to Severn. So straightened, the bay's true shoreline would stretch more than 8,000 miles. Scientists who measure such things have found that most lakes and coastal embayments have a shoreline that is two, three, or four times their length or width. But the Chesapeake Bay is unique, with a shoreline forty times its length.

This purely geophysical phenomenon of the bay's copious edge begets an intimacy between the Chesapeake and its peoples unrivaled along most of the planet's fringes. From Baltimore to Norfolk, the bay and its tidal tributaries touch our lives to a high degree. Extraordinary numbers of us are able to see it from our bridges and homes and parks and offices and to poke around in it on a daily basis. That is probably why, in Maryland, the state boat is an oyster skipjack, the state dog

*The old hunting lodge on Great Fox Island, now an environmental education center for the Chesapeake Bay Foundation, gets farther from land every year as erosion inexorably reduces the island.*

a Chesapeake Bay retriever, and the state university mascot a diamondback terrapin. Even the state fossil, *Ecphora quadricostata*, an extinct marine snail, was unearthed from the Calvert Cliffs along southern Maryland's bayshore. And if I had my way, both Maryland and Virginia would retire their respective state birds, the oriole and the cardinal, in favor of the great blue heron. That lordly sentinel of the marshy shallows is found in every county of both states wherever land and water merge, a living symbol of the edge wherein so much of both states' personality resides.

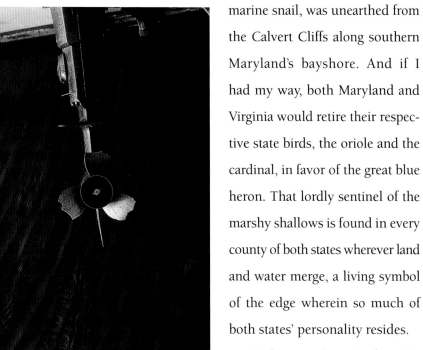

*The bay's bottom is seldom far from its surface, as many an outboard motor's propeller can attest. Any Chesapeake boater who has never run aground is either a liar or still tied to the dock.*

*(Facing) Water, water everywhere, but much of it is shallow. The bay is 200 miles long and up to 30 miles wide, but across hundreds of square miles, it is knee-deep or less.*

I take joy and wonder from the heron for many reasons, but most of all, I envy its perspective on the edge. It spends its days wriggling long toes in the warm, rich muck of the shallows, golden gimlet eyes spying out the camouflaged minnows and crabs. But in a few flaps of its great wings, it can soar to immense heights, and from here the margins of coiled land and water present a fundamental beauty.

This beauty lies in the curves and whorls, patterns so antidotal to the world of straight lines and right angles we have imposed across much of our landscape. Philosophers and physicists have theorized that for reasons as deeply rooted as the design of our own brains, the gentle, repetitive form of the curve delights our eye and stirs an almost sensual pleasure within us. Natural flows, whether rivers, glaciers, or melting frost on a windowpane, seldom run straight for long before they curve. Great minds, from Buckminster Fuller to Albert Einstein, have probed these phenomena; many theories exist to explain how meandering happens. But why? What makes these serpentine pathways such a preferred path of the universe? We are still as humbled as the writer of Proverbs 30:18, who listed among "things too wonderful for me to understand…the way of a serpent upon a rock."

More than ever I crave the times when I, flying in a small plane, like the heron can follow the bay's edges. The natural patterns there clash with the straight ditches gouged across the land behind them for farm drainage and mosquito control, with the squared-off designs of our plowing and paving. The ditch, the road, the site newly bulldozed for development, all are efficient in their narrow ways, but they are symbols of attitudes toward the earth that ultimately impoverish us.

*Going with the flow, Snuggles helps federal warden Mike Harrison patrol the serpentine tidal guts permeating Smith Island's Martin National Wildlife Refuge.*

From a heron's high view, these conflicting patterns seem a metaphor for the way we think, versus the way we ought to think.

The bay's edge is not only long, it is broad, though this is not immediately apparent. Once the land slips from sight beneath the waters of the bay and its tidal rivers, it slopes only very slightly in most places. Canoeing the broad, but deceptively thin waters around Smith Island, where I used to take schoolchildren on field trips for the Chesapeake Bay Foundation, my advice was always: "If you capsize, save your life—stand up!" The fact is, about 10 percent of the bay's entire 4,400-square-mile area is less than a meter deep,

and about 20 percent is less than two meters. This means that sunlight penetrates to the bottom across a great deal of the Chesapeake, enabling lush growths of submerged grasses that in effect extend the high-quality habitat and biological productivity of the visible edge far offshore.

All of these "edge" habitats—marsh and wetland forest and underwater meadow and tidal mud flat—make the fringes of the Chesapeake incredibly attractive to life. Just peer into the thigh-thick rolls of underwater grasses fetched up in the scrapes dragged by soft crabbers. The waterman is looking only for marketable crabs, which are drawn to the shelter of the grasses to shed their shells. But the grass also throbs with shrimp, snails, minnows, seahorses, worms, and the juvenile stages of a dozen kinds of important bay fishes. In the winter, the grasses are traditional food for more than a million ducks and geese and swans that collect on the Chesapeake from across North America. With their big paddle feet and long necks, the swans can reach and excavate the grasses in deeper water than other fowl; and one of winter's loveliest sights—increasingly scarce in these days of declines in both grasses and waterfowl—is a flotilla of swans, white as a snowbank against the marshy edge, surrounded by a raucous

*While a straight line is fastest, a river knows it is not always best. Sediment in the bends of this Eastern Shore creek forms marshes more richly productive than all the prime farmland on either side.*

A frozen cove glows with
the pastels of a winter
sunset. Protected nooks
like this ice over readily,
but only twice this century,
in the 1930s and the 1970s,
has the bay's main stem
frozen solid.

20

*Snowfall blots detail and emphasizes form: (above) the fantastic meandering of water through the Elliott Island salt marsh, (facing) the economical lines of a working waterman's skiff at Smith Island. The skiff's flat bottom and front decking give the dipnetter a podium from which to catch crabs in warmer times.*

retinue of half-a-dozen species of ducks feeding on the floating leftovers of the swans' vigorous rooting.

So much of the life we associate with the bay is more truly associated with the bay's edges. There, and not in the deeps or the bay mouth, is where you find herons, egrets, ibis, skimmers, and oyster catchers, and the nesting sites of ospreys and eagles. There, too, is where the young of rockfish and shad and herring congregate, safe in the thin water from bigger fish.

It is common in nature to find exceptional richness and diversity of life where two different natural regimes, like field and forest, or land and water, form an edge. I consider the intersections of the seasons a sort of edge, one that is alive with the migrating herds and flocks and schools of creatures, tugged along on the skirts of spring and autumn. Sometimes on the bay we get a double overlap of edges, and then something extraordinary can result. The regions around Smith and

Tangier islands in midbay are a prime example, where freshwater from the bay's head mingles just enough with the ocean at its mouth to achieve an average salinity that is very attractive to both male and female crabs (jimmies and sooks to the initiated). This inviting margin of salt and sweet, superimposed upon the vast marsh and grassy shallows of the region, makes one of the most preferred places on earth for *Callinectes sapidus*, the Chesapeake blue crab, to mate and shed its shell. Lawrence Durrell, the travel writer and essayist, once wrote that if you wiped the country of France clean of all its peoples and its history, the qualities of the landscape there would again inevitably produce Frenchmen. And the same might be said of the unique island crabbing cultures of the midbay: that if they did not exist, the powers of the edge there would again create them anew.

The great attraction of the edge for life has become in modern times a double-edged sword. It is a worldwide phenomenon that people, perhaps even more than wildlife, tend to gravitate to the coastlines. About 50 percent of everyone on earth lives on perhaps 5 percent of the land—and a great deal of that 5 percent is near the continental edges. In America, about two-thirds of the population is located in a narrow envelope less than 50 miles from an ocean or a Great Lakes coast. Not surprisingly, the natural edge has increasingly been filled, drained, paved, polluted, and straightened. The Chesapeake is no exception. Virginia during the last century is estimated to have lost nearly half its wetlands, Maryland nearly three-quarters. More than a thousand miles of bay shoreline have been "hardened" and straightened with the addition of bulkheads and riprap to protect development from erosion and storms. Thousands of acres of oyster bottoms have been closed because of the presence or threat of pollution from marinas and septic tanks installed too close to the edge.

We fail to heed the bitter irony of building more and more projects like Oyster Cove, a condo development in Maryland that necessitated dredging part of an oyster bar. Near the bay's head at Havre de Grace, Canvasback Cove condos recently opened, and no one at the celebration mentioned that it delivered one more blow to the scant remaining beds of underwater vegetation that once attracted millions of canvasback ducks to the Susquehanna Flats there.

In the right places, of course, waterfront development or redevelopment is arguably the highest and best use of the bay edge. Baltimore's

*When the tide swells and*
*the water perfectly reflects*
*the sky of a still May dawn,*
*the marsh seems to float,*
*suspended in equilibrium.*

Wind, such as this 50-plus-
knot squall announcing a
cold front, drives the bay
like few other forces. Wind
propels the tides above or
below normal; it affects
oxygen in the water and the
spawning success of crabs
and fish.

Inner Harbor, Norfolk's Waterside Mall, and similar, more modest efforts in smaller bay and riverside towns have revitalized lagging economies. But as human population in the bay region continues to swell, there is a growing realization that for all the natural edge that is left the beleaguered Chesapeake, it is past time to say, enough!

Legislation recently enacted and other bills now being debated to protect the shoreline have begun to promote appreciation of a vital and overlooked function of the natural edge. The forests and wetlands and submerged grasses, we are beginning to understand, are more than magnets for natural life, and more than places to contemplate the beauty of meanders. They are also key to what might be termed the estuary's *resilience*, its capacity to protect itself against both human and natural insult. Forests, for example, are proving unparalleled at filtering out and absorbing the pollutants in rainwater that wash to the bay from farms and developed lands. They also store water in wet periods, softening the impacts of flooding, and later release that water in

*(Facing) Three villages cling to the only patches of ground a few inches above sea level on Smith Island, 12 miles out in the bay. Tylerton is in the foreground, Rhodes Point in the upper left, and Ewell in the upper right.*

*(Above) "Main Street" in Tylerton is deserted on a June morning. Everyone is out crabbing here in the soft-crab center of the world.*

droughts, keeping streams flowing healthily. Wetlands and submerged grasses perform many similar functions. No pollution controls we can tack on to our alterations of the natural edge are a perfect—or even near-perfect—substitute.

Thus, maintaining all that is left of the bay's natural resistance to pollution is just as critical as spending billions for bigger sewage treatment plants—and the results are a sight prettier.

Even as we struggle to protect the margins of our estuary against assault from the land's side, it appears that something new and ominous is happening on the watery side of the edge. The erosion of the shoreline before waves and the land's submergence by a rising sea level have been happening on the Chesapeake since it was formed. Now, however, an industrialized world's combustion of fossil fuels promises to warm the climate and speed sea-level rise. Scientists estimate we are now undergoing an acceleration in the rate of rise from a foot a century to somewhere between two and seven feet by the year 2100. That may

*(Above and facing) At the turn of the century, Holland Island boasted several hundred citizens, two baseball diamonds, stores, and fine waterfront homes. Todds, Parkses, and Tylers settled the island more than 200 years ago, but by 1918 the last family had fled to the mainland. Now, even the last traces of human habitation are vanishing, victims of erosion and rising sea level.*

seem comfortably far off to most of us, but not to the watermen who live on the lovely and unique islands of Smith and Tangier and in a dozen other marsh-side fishing communities of the Chesapeake.

The same gentle slope of land and bay bottom that gives the Chesapeake so wonderfully broad a mergence of land and water will translate even a few inches of sea-level rise into an intrusion of water across several horizontal feet. Many a bay waterman has crabbed and clammed and oystered off a place in the middle bay known as Holland Island, and watched each year as the gravestones there fall into the water. Within living memory that island had streets lined with neat homes, stores, playgrounds, and churches. All are gone, banished by erosion around the second decade of the century. Though some islands may be doomed by rising sea levels, the mainland's edge may simply move inland before the sea's advance, if we are wise enough to quit developing to the very waterline and leave the bay some elbow room. This then is some of what the bay's edge is about— long and intimate, shallow and productive, a magnet for life—places of timeless beauty, and also places that in our lifetimes may vanish beneath the waves.

# BUFFERS AND WETLANDS

It was one of those mid-September afternoons on the Eastern Shore of Maryland when stubborn summer takes its parting shot. Temperature and humidity panted neck and neck toward the 90s, even as a cold front whistled down across the Appalachians. Seeking an unmarked country lane, I slowed the car to watch a farmer harvest the last of his corn. It made a pretty scene, a big square of grain radiant in the long slants of sun, sloping down to a silver bend of the Choptank River. A combine lumbered along the rows, munching stalks in neat swaths, pausing occasionally to regurgitate mounds of brassy kernel into waiting trucks—the very picture of order and productivity, a clear and satisfying accounting for months of effort. The soil had been amended with lime, invested with seed, supplied with precisely calculated quantities of fertilizer, and watered by diesel engines pumping water from the river. Pre- and postemergent pesticides were sprayed to make sure the land sang only in the key of corn. Now the reward: if the farmer was diligent, and the weather smiled, he might reap 150, even 200 bushels per acre—an example of modern agriculture's astounding annual performance that feeds all of America on the bounty produced by 2 percent of us, with enough left over to accrue tens of billions of export dollars.

I found my turnoff and prepared for what seemed by comparison a trivial evening's work, recording the night sounds in the tidal marsh at Kings Creek for a Chesapeake Bay Foundation slide show. What a difference a foot or so of elevation makes, I thought as I passed a thin break of forest separating tillable farmland from the boggy, near-impassable marsh. Through the trees a different world unfolded. Kings Creek, encompassing more than a square mile, is a classic meander marsh, a great lozenge of wetlands situated between looping bends of the Choptank. It receives, on both incoming and outgoing tides, sediment carried by the river and slung by centrifugal force to the outside of the bends. The sediments are both fertilizer and building material for the marsh, which must constantly accumulate them to keep pace with a sea level that has been slowly rising since the end of the last Ice Age. In the past 4,000 years since the newly formed

*The bay country's extensive mergences of land and water are more than just home to birds such as the lordly great blue heron. Forested swamps and wetlands form a superb filter, buffering waterways against pollution from farms and development.*

Chesapeake first created it, the marsh here has used its river-borne gift of silt to build, inch by inch, nearly 14 feet higher as the still-rising seas continually try to submerge it.

I have heard ditch diggers and stream channelizers wonder why rivers hardly ever run naturally straight, as that would more efficiently drain water. Such byproducts of the river's meandering as Kings Creek marsh remind us that there is more purpose to nature than maximizing her hydraulic capacity. Indeed, as the 21st century approaches, we humans are still painfully working through how to value and compare the outputs of the marsh with that of the cornfield, how to equate

*American three-square rushes, spatterdock lilies, and floating duckweed share a freshwater wetland. Drainage and development have destroyed tens of thousands of acres of such places across the Chesapeake region.*

the natural and the manufactured. It is far from just an academic or philosophical issue. The lack of such understanding directly underlies the nation's filling and draining and paving of more than half its original 200 million acres of wetlands in the lower 48 states. Similar losses have occurred in the Chesapeake watershed. The marsh-loss trends have slowed in recent years, but remain headed downward, despite pronouncements of "no net loss" by politicians.

Value appears so much easier to calculate in the cornfield. All the energy, from human labor to chemical manufacture, is focused on maximizing corn. The price the crop fetches, as well as the goods and services employed in producing it, are in turn dutifully recorded as contributions to the Gross National Product (GNP), a primary way the government measures our nation's prosperity.

In the marsh, nothing is so straightforward. The place is a riot of tangled, muted color, lush greens and paler golds in nuances enough to dither the palette of any landscape painter. It is a shame one of the lustier impressionists like Gauguin never set brush to capturing the atmosphere of a place like Kings Creek. Big cordgrass and phragmites reeds, spiky seed heads and plumes tossing on the humid evening breeze,

*Duckweed richly carpets the still waters of an oxbow in the cypress swamps along the Pocomoke River. The Pocomoke winds upstream from the bay nearly to the Atlantic Ocean.*

sprout from the rich black muck to heights approaching 12 feet. Cattails, swollen fat and brown as Cuban cigars, form another tier of growth. Along the capillary waterways that pervade the marsh, the big-leaved tuckahoe plants are producing the spicy berries so loved by wood ducks. Waterhemp, which swells in the space of a few months from seed to young tree, producing up to a quart of seed per plant, is beginning to keel over from its own weight. Boneset, a twining vine studded with delicate white flowers, crawls over everything.

There is a feeling here to the late-summer vegetation almost of debauchery, of everything having fed so well and long on the broth of muck and tidal flow that the marsh has grown paunchy and overindulged and must now collapse, spent. Seeds and fruits and burst pods of ample variety are strewn carelessly everywhere. They will end up being harvested by everything from snapping

turtles to muskrats, from minnows to whole symphonies of migrating songbirds. The tons of vegetation will weather, decay, and ultimately be broken down by bacteria into a rich, organic stew. Flushed from the marsh, these nutrients will help fuel webs of life in the Choptank and the Chesapeake, extending from plankton to rockfish, and on to eagles and humans who both love the flesh of the rock.

Dusk is falling when I encamp at the marsh's center, reachable only because a nature group has constructed a narrow boardwalk. A blizzard of red-winged blackbirds swirls there, thousand upon thousand, massing preparatory to southward migration. They settle into the tall reeds with a roar, like the hard gusts of wind that get your attention even in the midst of a gale. Full dark quiets the red-wing storm, but it is nearly midnight before distant noises—barking dogs, feed-grinding augers in chicken houses across the river, and passing Salisbury-to-Baltimore commuter traffic—have fallen away enough to turn on the supersensitive microphone and get the "clean" sounds of nature they like in the audio lab. Through the earphones, the marsh comes alive. The water coursing in and out through its muddy intestines is a constant medley of "pocks" and

*The long shadows of a summer morning fall across Dragon Run, headwaters of the Piankatank River. This extraordinary freshwater wetland has been protected largely through conservationists' efforts.*

*Clean and clear, rainwater flows from the dense vegetation that acts as a purifying green sponge wherever it remains along the edges of creeks and rivers feeding the bay.*

"smacks" and delicate kisses as minnows glean detritus and insects from its surface; occasionally comes the crash of something big—bass? raccoon? muskrat? And then, after a brief silence, the pockers and kissers resume.

Several birds are about, and I suppose most readers would be fooled were I to name them by matching their calls with the tortured renditions in my *Audubon* guidebooks. Suffice it to say that I heard a yowler, a wheeper, a croaker, a ponker, and a hooter, and they went on for most of the night. With daylight, a whole new cast of characters— wrens, blackbirds, hawks, and waterfowl—came on stage. Should I go there in a different season, a whole different play would be running.

There is productivity in such a marsh to match or exceed that of any cornfield, but the marsh's genius is to nourish life in astounding diversity, rather than to astonish with a single harvest. The GNP seems confused by the fact that all this natural productivity comes for free; that it just happens, over and over, millennia after millennia. We do nothing to receive this annual king's ransom in fish and fowl and beauty and diversity. The GNP is positively affronted by the thought, and it does not accord any value at all to wetlands like Kings Creek marsh. Curiously, if we were to

*Fiddlehead ferns thrive in the cool damp of the region's lowland hardwood forests, a type of habitat with little protection outside of publicly owned lands.*

destroy it—drain it for growing corn or fill it for a shopping mall—then GNP, which neither adds nature's benefits nor subtracts them when destroyed, would finally count the site as a plus for the nation. Similarly, a cut and harvested forest boosts the GNP, while a living, functioning forest preserve does not. And the pristine waters of Prince William Sound in Alaska never contributed so much to the GNP as when Exxon spent billions there to clean up their oil spill.

A damselfly maintains a delicate balance on a stalk of aquatic grass in the interior of the Zekiah Swamp, a labyrinth of woods and water south of Washington, D.C., where Abraham Lincoln's assassin once sought to lose pursuers.

It is easy to make sport of the GNP, but the implications of its blindness are sobering. We tend to perpetuate and increase what we value, and though we see ourselves as loving nature, we don't value it in ways that count. Some fundamental insights to the problem come from the emerging discipline of ecological economics, through which a number of respected economists and ecologists are trying to forge a method for valuing both natural and human systems. They attach high value in a system, natural or human, to the concept of sustainability. The GNP, by contrast, sees good only in growth. Sustainability, the ecological economists say, does not have anything to do with pessimistic notions of a stagnant, no-growth economy; rather it means continued development and consumption, *but development and consumption that does not eat into capital*. We easily grasp that concept as applied to our individual finances. Living off one's investments is not sustainable if you are spending more than the interest earned, and dipping into your capital. But the concept of valuing economic activity that preserves and enhances natural capital—our base inheritance of forests and wetlands and quality waters—remains an intellectual abstraction.

Among the natural capital banked under wet-lands, Kings Creek marsh is an attention-getter, a nifty way to dramatize the need for better ways to value our planet. It is representative of the best of our wetlands—world class in productivity and higher than average in diversity and size. It has been recognized as an extraordinary Chesapeake Bay wetland by the Smithsonian as long ago as 1974, and much of it is now protected forever, incorporated within the Nature Conservancy's permanent holdings. This is all good; but how we treat our champions, our elite natural areas, may not be a true benchmark for progress in learning to properly value the whole blue ball of wax we call earth.

Beavers, which have left their signature on this wetland hardwood, have shaped the hydrology of North America with their dam building more than any species—save perhaps the Army Corps of Engineers.

For example, fierce debates currently rage over how much, if any, protection to extend to hundreds of thousands of acres of wetlands spread across the bay region. Many are not the classic tidal marsh system. They are bogs and ponds and sloughs of the interior. Some are small and

A spider, part of the diversity of life in freshwater wetlands, nets the morning dew along Kings Creek off the Choptank River.

(Facing) Bronze copper butterflies sup from curly milkweed pods at Kings Creek, where the Nature Conservancy has preserved 250 acres, complete with 2,000 feet of observation walkways. It is accessible by canoe.

Salt-marsh snails, peri-winkles climb the stalks of spartina grass, elevating up and down in perfect synchrony with the flood and ebb of the tides.

isolated, occupying less than an acre. Some are not wet year-round, or even every year, but may be classed wetlands because certain vegetation qualifies their underlying soils as "hydric." These do not host great flights of spectacular waterfowl. Some are, in my humble opinion, ugly and nondescript. "Is This A Wet-land?" asks a flyer published to aid identification of some of the more obscure wetlands: "Are the bases of the trees swollen? Do the leaves on the ground look mat-ted, washed with silt, grayer than those on adjacent sites? Are bottles and cans lying on the site filled with mud? Are there leaves or trashy debris that look like they've been washed up against roots?" Nothing here would inspire Sidney Lanier to write the epic "Marshes of Glynn." One of the problems, it seems, in comparing natural capital to financial capital is that the former comes in a dizzying variety of denominations and currencies, and sometimes doesn't even look to us like any-thing we'd want to bank.

In fact, science increasingly is making the case that even the lowliest and most ephemerally soggy of our wetlands have real value. Some of the tiniest spots, by virtue of their very isolation, act as oases harboring rare and endangered species of plants and animals. A broader case is made for virtually all wetland soils as superior natural buffers, damping the extremes of flood and drought, and filtering pollutants from rainwater before it runs into waterways.

This case for natural wetlands as pollution buffers, as part of the bay's natural resilience, is an increasingly powerful influence on how we value land. And forests, it is turning out, have similar capacities. Water-quality monitoring on creeks whose watersheds are forested shows dramatically better water, across the board, than creeks whose watersheds are dominated by either agriculture or development. We can, in fact, apply this broad statement to the Chesapeake's 64,000-square-mile watershed: *any lands left in their natural, vegetated state are better for the bay than any lands altered by human enterprise.*

Some might call that a declaration of war, or just plain suicide. Wetlands cover only a few percent of the watershed, and current efforts to protect just that relative smidgen promise a donnybrook among landowners and environmental regulators for years to come. Indeed, earlier fights begun to protect our air and water were in retrospect easy. From the start it was "our" air and "our" water—the common good; how dare any individual or corporation presume to pollute them? But in extending more value to land in its undisturbed state, we are taking quite a leap. "Our" air and water, surely, but more often than not, "my" land, "private" property, "individual" rights. In fact, it is "your" land, but connected, irrevocably as water flows downhill, to "our" bay.

So what are we saying here? Nationalize the watershed? Halt all agriculture and new development? Such prospects are neither possible nor desirable. But do recognize that the natural landscape—all of it, and not just its more ecologically spectacular manifestations—is our vital, irreplaceable, and generally unimprovable natural capital. Recognize that the ways in which we currently use land, whether for agriculture or development, and often even for relatively benign uses such as forestry, inevitably degrade that natural capital. Recognize that the stated goals of federal and state governments for the bay are not only to halt current environmental declines but to *restore* it to at least its health of a few decades past.

It is not pie in the sky to think of a broader value for land. More environmentally benign systems of agriculture are already being embraced and moving into the mainstream; we have the expertise and technology to house ourselves and conduct our commerce with dramatically less impact on the natural landscape. The goal must be for all human activities on the land to leave it functioning as closely as possible to its natural state, and to be as conservative about altering natural capital as we would in spending ours and our children's life savings. What it comes back to is a question of values.

*Brandishing their big, but fairly harmless claws, fiddler crabs scuttle across a tidal mud flat. Densities of fiddlers, choice prey for many birds of the salt marsh, can reach millions per acre, a small part of what has been called the bay's "great protein factory."*

The common toad, which has family on every continent except Australia, relies on camouflage for protection during a sunbath.

(Facing) Few species of plants can survive in saltwater, resulting in little plant diversity in salt marshes. Needlerush forms the vast monoculture that dominates the mid-Chesapeake salt marshes as the prairie once did the American Midwest.

# MAN'S IMPRINT

Come. I'm going to guide you to one of those rare, hidden nooks of the bay country where nature still appears as glorious and untrammeled as it did a thousand years ago. It is where Dave and I have gathered some of the most spectacular pictures for this book. Our point of departure for the trip might be enough to satisfy most appetites for unspoiled scenery. It is the Eastern Shore village of Bivalve, near the mouth of the Nanticoke—a river that is, along with the Pocomoke and the Rappahannock, the most pristine among the tributaries of the Chesapeake.

It is chilly, mid-March, long before dawn. No breeze ripples the slatey calm of the bay. Only the wild, lost hallooing of swans preparing to migrate north and the occasional sassing of a mallard break the silence. For the next half an hour by fast boat, you'll see little but the black of the bay, edged here and there by even blacker lines of salt marsh. First light is seeping westward, tinting just the crests of our wake mauve and silver, and showing the outlines of a low-lying island. Just short of bumping a wall of needlerush marsh, we find a hidden tidal gut and follow it deep into the island.

*A lone fishing skiff seems insignificant on the broad Susquehanna, source of nearly half the bay's fresh-water; but well over a million sportfishermen visit the bay annually, and the need to limit how much they catch is becoming obvious.*

We kill the motor and let a mud flat quench our remaining forward speed. Nearby, great wings flail the cool air like flapping bedsheets. A rasping, croaking, and clacking surrounds us. Bony, elongate reptilian creatures, elemental and stark as runes against the rising sun, are stirring in the boughs of dead trees. It is the dawn of the day—the dawn of time it could be out here, where a brontosaur munching in the marsh would not seem so out of place. Here is where the ancient-wings gather to mate and nest and rear their young. Arriving every year close to Valentine's Day, they are the first species to call winter's bluff in this region.

The true and literal "ancient wing" was archaeopteryx, a crow-sized, feathered dinosaur that lived and feebly flew 130 million years ago, the forerunner of all modern birds. The great blue herons that hold the franchise on this island have not changed greatly since their family, the Ardeidae, which includes egrets and bitterns, evolved some 60 million years back. They retain more of the reptilian archaeopteryx than most birds in their guttural language and the ptero-

dactyl-like figure they cut. To my mind, ancient-wing suits them fine.

On their perches, the ancient-wings stretch and bow to one another; they slowly rub chestnut-splotched thighs, male against female, and gently touch together great marlinespikes of beaks. In the meeting of beaks, it happens on occasion that their plumed breasts simultaneously touch, and their glossy necks, curving fluidly between chest and beak form the almost-perfect heart shape of a valentine. Ornithologists have long since tried to take all the romance out of such observation, categorizing the heron's stances into "stretch display," "snap display," "full forward and aggressive upright displays," and the like. What I have described is no doubt recorded in some scholarly field note as the "recurved proboscis stance." Nonetheless, watching them touch and rub and gaze steadfastly into one another's eyes, it is easy to imagine that something more than instinct beats in heron hearts this day.

The sun has risen higher now, and the marsh basks in it, golden amid the sparkling blue of the bay. Terrapin heads dot the surface of the tidal gut, hobnobbing after a long winter buried in the cold mud. High above an osprey flutters, treading air and peeping furiously for his affianced to

*Thomas Point Light near the mouth of the South River, built in 1875, was until 1986 the bay's last manned lighthouse. It remains in operation, though automated.*

*(Above and facing) Hardy swimmers embark from Sandy Point for Kent Island, where the bay narrows down to nearly four miles across. During the annual Bay Bridge Swim in June, they fight currents which on occasion have made boat rescues necessary.*

pay attention to this ageless courtship ritual known as sky dancing. The electric vibrato of swamp sparrows' calling hums through the rushes. Here, 75 miles from downtown Washington, at the center of a hundred-mile radius containing millions of people, time seems arrested; human influence appears no more than when Captain

John Smith sailed these solitudes in 1608.

It is a nice fiction at any rate, and on mornings like this I almost believe it. But new wings already are glinting high above the ancient-wings. We have to leave, and quickly, because as they do almost every day, the warplanes are coming to bomb and strafe the island, which belongs to the

U.S. Navy. Perhaps later in the week destroyers will practice lobbing their big shells into the place, too. There is solitude and wilderness here alright, but it is bought by bombs. Virtually all human intrusion, from fishermen and duck hunters to overflights by nonmilitary aircraft, is prohibited by law and by the hazards of unexploded ordinance deposited here over the years.

The herons, half a mile or more from the target area, seem not to mind the planes and bombs. I don't believe, from my own observations, that they hear well, relying more on keen sight. Many of their nests here are government issue—federal replacements for the nesting trees taken out by an errant napalm strike a few decades ago. This spring, every artificial nesting platform over-flowed with chicks, reaffirming our island as one of the larger and more successful colonies of ancient-wings on the East Coast.

Are there lessons here about humans and nature? Do we environmentalists really want to confront them? Answers in a minute; but first, come: I'm going to guide you to another of my special places, high up in the bay's drainage basin, where the fishing for native trout is every bit as good as the birdwatching on our marsh island.

I must admit that Spring Creek, a coldwater

freshet that ambles 24 miles through the folds of field and forest quilting Centre County, Pennsylvania, is not quite the trout water it was in pristine days. An old-timer recalls a typical expedition there in 1927. He caught trout all evening out of a single pool, keeping only five. They weighed 27 pounds. By the mid-1970s the creek, heavily fished and increasingly subjected to pollution, had devolved into your basic "put and take" trout stream— stocked each spring from state hatcheries and lined bank to bank by eager anglers who quickly caught virtually all these semidomesticated trout. Since then, Spring Creek has miraculously blossomed with native trout, big and wild. It is the top trout stream in a state renowned for its trout fishing, and maybe tops in the East. The definition of "Class A"

*(Above and facing) All manner of power and sail craft find the creeks around Annapolis prime dockage. Recreational boating nearly tripled on the Chesapeake between 1967 and 1990.*

trout water is 45 pounds of trout per acre. A 12-mile stretch of Spring Creek in 1988 measured 150 pounds per acre.

Was the miracle behind the comeback a renewed dedication to pollution control? Not really. In fact, pollution from agriculture and

(Facing) Sprawling development across the bay's watershed is consuming farms, forests, and open space at a rate more than triple that of 1950, when people lived more compactly in cities and towns.

(Above) Growing grain increasingly cannot yield the quick returns that come from seeding the land in suburbs. Development competes directly for the level, well-drained soils of prime farmland.

Oyster tongers harvest a declining bounty in front of the new Oyster Cove condominiums at Kent Island.

The marina for the condos necessitated dredging part of the oyster bar there.

development is a growing threat that could some-day wipe out the creek's gains if not checked. Spring Creek's comeback began when two ex-tremely toxic chemicals, kepone and mirex, were found to have leaked into the creek from a waste la-goon. The creek is posted for most of its length with toxic warnings, forbidding the keeping of any fish caught. With heavy fishing pressure thus removed, within a few years the native population surged back to levels that recalled the good old days.

We could tour other places far from the Chesapeake and see paradoxes similar to our creek protected by kepone and our marsh island preserved by bombs. A wildlife refuge of sig-nificant proportions is the demilitarized zone between the two Koreas. Similar land-mined ground around the Berlin Wall before it fell was alive with wildlife. No man's land turns out to be everything else's land. The point is not that explo-sives and chemicals are good for nature; rather that we often underestimate how pervasive are the impacts on the natural world from the subtle, everyday consequences of our living and working and farming and recreating—in other words, just from our *being*.

For example, for more than a decade I have visited several heron nesting sites on remote Smith Island. All are 12 miles from the mainland, sur-rounded by thousands of acres of marsh and millions of acres of open bay. With a human population of around 500 on the island, herons easily outnumber people. Yet even here, there is significantly less nesting of the great blues in the sites only a mile or so from the island villages, compared to those that are a few miles distant (the latter also lie within a federal refuge that covers part of the island). The closer nesting colonies are hardly subjected to what we would consider great stress—the passing of watermen's boats, an occa-sional asparagus hunter from the villages, a few fishermen—but it seems to make a difference. These places are still full of nesting water birds, but they tend to be the great egrets, which by nature tolerate human intrusion much more than herons. Thus it seems possible that in our bombing range, a weekly traffic of birdwatchers, gentle souls every one, might ultimately be more disruptive to the herons than the Navy's bombing.

So badly we always want to discover the toxic bullet, the mystery pollutant, the outrageous in-dustrial polluter that is pushing nature over the edge—millions of us, all fervently wanting the problem to be anything but the simple presence of millions of us. What we need, with 15 million

*"Yellow boy," highly acidic runoff from coal mining, coats this Pennsylvania stream's bottom. The acid content kills all plant life in the water, leaving it crystal clear but barren.*

*(Facing) Oil from a small spill spreads a rainbow across an industrial corner of the Chesapeake. Although the potential for oil-tanker crackups commands more public attention, spills from land-based accidents add tens of thousands of gallons of oil to bay waters.*

people now living within the six-state watershed of the Chesapeake, is broader thinking about how humans impinge on and relate to the bay's natural systems. We need it fast, because another few million are moving here to join us in the next twenty or thirty years. From the widespread declines that have plagued the bay and many of its fish and fowl in recent years, we know we already are having too great an impact. We are committed to reducing that—but it must be reduced by enough to also totally offset that next few million of us. Otherwise we are likely to find ourselves in the classic dilemma of making cars or factories twice as clean, but meanwhile doubling the number of them.

I doubt it oversimplifies much to say that the majority of the public living around the bay sees the estuary's major problems as factories and sewage. These are good starting points, but a danger in stopping with such overt villains is it leads to thinking that overt and often technical repairs will be enough to restore and sustain the damaged Chesapeake ecosystem. To illustrate why that is not enough, let us examine some of the more identifiable impacts of our everyday living in the watershed of the bay. Although there are more of us around than in our parents' day, an even greater change has occurred in the space we each take up. I don't mean we are physically taller or heavier than Mom and Dad; but in our appetites for natural resources, we are comparative giants.

For example, families moving into the bay region in 1990 used, on average, nearly four times the open space per capita to house themselves as they did in 1950. This reflects smaller families living on sprawling suburban lots, versus the more compact settlement patterns—in cities and towns—that had been the norm. Such sprawl is the enemy of preserving farmland and forest, and sets up commuting patterns that generate far more energy use. The added public costs of serving sprawl—roads and utilities and schools and police services—run to hundreds of millions per year in Maryland alone. The impacts of sprawling across the landscape instead of living compactly reverberate endlessly: nearly twice as much sediment flowing into the water from land development; twice as much water use; twice as much air pollu-

tion from increased auto use. How many of us live around the bay is crucial to its health; but even more crucial is *how* each of us lives.

There are many practical changes we can make, such as wiser land-use policies, to decrease our impacts on nature while still living well; but this will not happen to a sufficient degree unless we also reexamine the fundamental bases of our flawed relations with the Chesapeake environment. Ann Woodlief, who has written presciently about Virginia's James River (*In River Time*, Algonquin Books), suggests we have not polluted so much through "mistake…a little 'oops' here, there and everywhere" as we have through being true to some basic attitudes toward nature. These attitudes are abundantly expressed in the metaphors we use in writing and speaking.

From the first day of colonial settlement, the lands and waters of the bay were seen as "storehouses" of exploitable wealth. To read description after description of the Chesapeake region by early explorers is to read one long shopping list. From early on, we also saw the James, Woodlief points out, as an adversary, a force to be tamed, regulated, combatted, and bent to our will; and today we still favor images of pollution as something we battle or wage war on. We desperately need new images and

*Power plants like Three Mile Island on the Susquehanna River and other industrial facilities congregate around the edge of the bay and its rivers for the economy of waterborne transport and to quench their immense thirst for cooling water.*

60

metaphors: living sustainably, respecting natural integrity, and, most radical of all, prescription for some areas—letting nature alone.

The Native Americans along the James never named the river. Naming it was the first thing the settlers did. Nowadays that carries over into a tendency to analyze nature in lieu of acting conservatively to protect it. I hear that any year now, we will be able to model the workings of the Chesapeake Bay on supercomputers, the implication being that having finally reduced the ecosystem to a mathematical certainty, cleanup of its waters can really get going.

It is hard to find fault with such projects, because they can save time and make pollution control more cost effective; but we rely on them overmuch. Nothing in a computer model of the Chesapeake gets at the absolutely fundamental need to respect the bay. To the contrary, there is an implicit expectation that once we comprehend the system down to the last data bit, we will then know exactly how far we can push it and exploit it.

A powerful and long-lived image of the Chesapeake that thwarts our efforts to coexist with the bay is the myth of inexhaustible bounty. It is powerful because in fact the bay has always been a bountiful place. The stories of early discov-erers about fish so abundant they virtually leapt into the boat are probably true, but consider for a moment what that might *not* mean about bounty.

Remember that in colonial days, fishing devices were small-scale and crude, and the number of fishermen, both natives and Europeans, was small. Therefore the pristine Chesapeake, though it contained huge quantities of seafood, also did not have seafood extraction occurring on a large scale. To remain brimful of fish, it need not have been so hugely productive of new ones every year as we assume.

In the final analysis, the toxic trout stream and the island of great bombed herons are curiosities that give us no useful pattern for a better accommodation between humans and the rest of nature. But these unreal corners of the watershed make us face a certain reality: that the old assumptions about our imprint on nature simply won't do if all that is still wild and beautiful is to survive.

*(Facing and above) At a cost of nearly $1 billion, the Washington, D.C. region has built a sewage treatment plant at Blue Plains on the Potomac to reduce some key pollutants by more than 99 percent. The river has responded with more fish, waterfowl, and underwater grass beds.*

*Harnessing the flow of the bay's biggest river, the 110-foot dam at Conowingo on the Susquehanna generates valuable hydroelectric power. Since 1928, it has also blocked the springtime surges of shad and herring that once ran as far as New York State to spawn. A new fish lift now attempts to restore the traditional migration.*

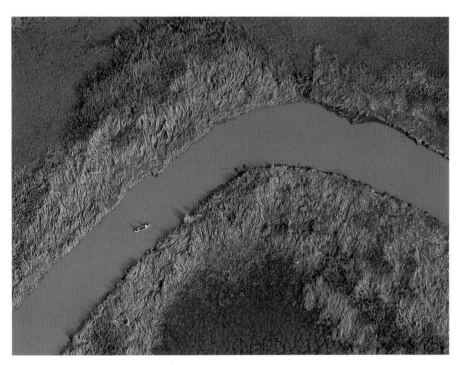

(Above and facing) Land clearing has made the bay extremely vulnerable to pollution from millions of tons of sediment carried by rainwater. Sediment smothers oyster beds, eliminates the light needed by underwater grasses, and damages the gills of young fish. It fills navigational channels, necessitating expensive dredging.

(Above, facing, and pages 70-71) Where agriculture encroaches too closely on the edge of the bay and its tributaries, it can be as harmful as any industrial or residential development. Animal wastes are a growing source of the pollutants that have killed underwater grasses and reduced oxygen in the bay.

# HARVESTING THE BOUNTY

Crab and oyster—that is the perfunctory answer you will often get as to what the watermen of the Chesapeake Bay mainly do. You might as well say that Van Gogh, in painting the French countryside, mainly used a couple of bright colors. The stew of life inhabiting coastal estuaries like the Chesapeake— places where rivers mix with the sea—is rich out of all proportion to the size of these minor and brackish indentations in the vast coastlines of North America. Whether measured by weight or by value, around three-quarters of all commercial and recreational fish, crabs, and shellfish caught in the United States are dependent at some stage of life on estuaries. Not surprisingly, a closer look at all the ways evolved to harvest such places reveals the complexity and subtlety that moved the late Gilbert Byron to write of the oystermen who left no record on their fluid environment though they worked there a lifetime:

*Men who never wrote a line*
*Are the greatest poets ever*
*Verses of love inscribed upon*
*The bottom of the cove.*

The bottom, except in the bay's extreme shallows, is forever unseen; yet it is a living entity to the waterman, who may spend his life focused intently on this invisible hunting ground. By summer, soft crabbers scrape the grassy shallows where the crabs shed. Others attack the bottom with hydraulic water jets, cutting trenches to dislodge the deeply buried maninose, or softshell clam. Down by the bay's mouth, a fleet of diesel-powered workboats rakes the bottom with big-toothed steel dredges for the pregnant crabs that bury themselves there each winter before spawning. Others pursue buried treasure on the bay's oyster "rocks," so-called because until dredging by large schooners and steam-powered vessels tore them apart more than a century ago, the oysters grew naturally in reefs large enough to impede navigation. Oystermen probe the bottom with tongs, both hand powered and hydraulic, and by dredging that now is limited mainly to the sail power of century-old skipjacks.

Many would argue there is no prettier sight connected to harvesting the bay than a skipjack "licking" across the rock, hoping to taste oysters below. My vote, however, goes to the lone

*The essential shallowness of the Chesapeake Bay— average depth around 20 feet—means that light can reach the bottom to grow vast meadows of submerged vegetation, which in turn offers refuge to soft crabs shedding their shells.*

dipnetter, perched on the very bow-tip of his graceful skiff, intent as a stalking heron on the shallow grass flats across which he propels himself with the bow of a 12-foot crab net. He comes to the flats in late summer, when the crabs are "doubled up," male and female cradled together, more intent on mating than evasive action. Leaning on his dipnet to shove the skiff now this way, now that, the netter seems to be dancing a languid waltz with his pole, and the skiff follows every move like a thing alive. On calm, cloudy days when the light is soft, conditions for netting are ideal. Sky and sea merge in a steel blue monochrome, and crabber and dipnet and skiff appear to dance their homage to the crab and the bay bottom suspended in midair.

Whether they scrape it, rake it, tong it, trench it, or probe it in graceful solitude with a dipnet, I think the bottom is, to the best of the bay's harvesters, something they can "see" in a way most of us will never understand. It may be similar to the way some Eskimo hunters have evolved a remarkable ability to orient themselves in the featureless and trackless Arctic. Once I spent a day in winter with an expert dipnetter, who said he

*(Facing) Chesapeake watermen have evolved unique boats and gear to harvest the "softies" which thrive in the bay's grass meadows. (Above) Hands that have held many a crab check for a telltale reddish tinge on the rear swim fin that forecasts the creature's readiness to shed into the highly valued soft crab.*

could spot the sign where diamondback terrapin had buried in the bottom of a cove. In the same way he dipped doubler crabs in summer, he could gouge the terrapin from their hibernation. In two hours of intense peering into the shallow water, I never saw a thing. Accidentally, I caught one terrapin. My friend, standing four feet away from me in the skiff, had by that time dipped more than 100.

Different watermen, even in the same fishery, relate differently to the bottom. Among oyster dredgers, there are those captains adept at dredging the edges along the drop-offs of channels. Others are known for how they can catch oysters on muddy bottom, while still others shine at working shelly bottom. Edward Harrison and his brother Daniel, retired skipjack captains from Smith Island, were renowned for working "hills" and could play more variations than a Bach fugue in working such oystery spots with just the precise combinations of speed, angle of attack, and length of cable paid out so as to load the dredges brimful.

More subtle still, but separating the best

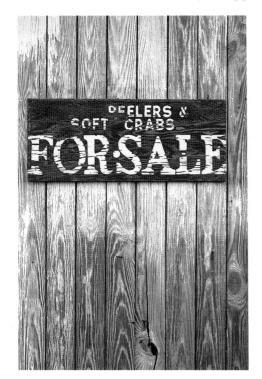

Crisfield ships soft crabs nationwide and as far as Japan. Peelers, hard crabs close to shedding their shells, are the prime bait for Chesapeake sportfishermen. (Facing) Dwight Marshall, a Smith Island soft crabber, nets doublers, flipping two coupled crabs high to separate male from female. The female is either soft or soon to be that way—a prerequisite for mating.

watermen from the rest, is mental attitude. Edward, whose boat the *Ruby Ford* was for decades a top catcher among the dredging fleet, says he hardly went to bed any night of the long, cold season without thinking about the day ahead, where he would go, and how he would dredge. I have often seen younger watermen stay home when the weather is nasty and the catches are scarce, calculating their catch would not cover expenses. The best harvesters look at it differently: if you do go out, you are always more likely to catch something than if you don't.

Harvesting the water can be reduced to two essential forms of capture, nets and traps (also called pots). Of the former, there are fyke nets, pound nets, seine nets, and gill nets, just to name the major ones; and many variations within these: anchored, staked, and drifted gill nets, for example. Becoming truly proficient with even one of these subcategories can be the work of a lifetime. Traps come in an equal variety: bank trap, swimmer trap, fish pot, crab pot, and—quite illegally, but a few still exist—duck traps. I find it intriguing to think of the bay as a wonderful mystery box into which you can dip any one of these hundreds of arrangements of meshes, and depending on what you use to sieve its waters, come up with different

*Work in the shanty continues for hours after a long day on the water harvesting soft crabs. (Top) Ed Harrison sorts his softies into sizes: whales, jumbos, primes, hotels, and mediums (no such thing as smalls). (Above) Dwight Marshall "fishes up," removing newly shed crabs from his holding tanks before they can draw chemicals from the bay-water to reform a hard shell.*

pictures of what lives there. Even slight variations on a theme can yield dramatically different results. Both a crab pot and a bank trap, for example, are essentially wire-mesh boxes that trap life by inviting it into a cone-shaped entryway. Once it emerges from the small end of the cone, it cannot get back out. But a crab pot catches mostly crabs, and a bank trap also gets terrapins, eels, occasional rockfish, and horseshoe crabs. And slightly smaller mesh in a crab pot will quite successfully catch only peelers, those crabs ready to shed their shells, but will be avoided by hard crabs.

If I were commissioned to portray a Chesapeake Bay waterman through art, my masterpiece would be a sculpture: rusty dredges for feet, oysters and crabs sprouting from between iron toes; oyster tongs for one leg and a long-handled crabnet for the other. A jumble of wire-mesh traps would be the basic building blocks for his head and body, with part of a skipjack's mast to give him spine; and the whole caboodle swathed and fleshed with the diamond meshes of a dozen kinds of net. The hydraulic hose off a clamming rig would make him a good right arm; for the left a stout diesel crankshaft, and bushel baskets for hands. Saltwater would swish continuously through the whole creation, for the best harvesters keep the bay running through their minds as well as their gear. I don't suppose such a creation would be considered pretty, but if thrown overboard, boy, what it wouldn't catch!

Even as we celebrate the richness of ways we harvest the Chesapeake, we must acknowledge ominous trends in the bounty on which it is based. In only the last quarter century, these are the facts: commercial catches of rockfish have declined from traditional levels by 80 percent in Virginia and 65 percent in Maryland; American shad, once as much a premier sport and commercial fish here as the rock, is down by 60 percent in Virginia and 90 percent in Maryland. Maryland has banned all fishing for the shad. The list continues: hickory shad, down 96 percent baywide; alewife and blueback herring, down 92 percent. The population of the oyster, staple of the bay's harvest for more than a century, is estimated to be as little as one percent of the shellfish that covered the bay bottom a hundred years ago.

The reasons cover the map: pollution, loss of habitat, disease, overfishing by both sport and commercial interests, and a history of weak or misguided management by government agencies and legislatures. Those who would soft-pedal the situation note correctly that not every species is

down. Harvests of the resilient blue crab have held at near-record levels throughout the past decade, and menhaden, netted commercially by the millions of pounds in Virginia waters, continue healthily. Bluefish, an important sport species, provided ample fishing during many years during the 1980s.

Many watermen hold to a deep belief in natural cycles. They and their forefathers have known times like the year in the 1920s when the best rockfish netter on the bay, Captain Irving Crouch of Rock Hall, a man who measured weekly success by the ton, fished hard all winter and caught only a single striper. And Smith Islanders, who live in the heart of the bay's best crabbing grounds,

*Noodles, a shanty cat, dines daily on soft crabs that would cost several dollars apiece in a mainland restaurant. Cats outpopulate people on Smith Island by perhaps three to one.*

*Bushel of crabs, bushel of oysters, bushel of terrapins: the venerable wooden bushel basket remains the measure of choice for packaging the Chesapeake's seafood.*

I. T. Todd, a Crisfield seafood packer, is one of the
last surviving natives of
Holland Island, now nearly
eroded beneath the waves.
He steams crabs 30 bushels
at a time.

abandoned their homes for shipyard jobs in the city during World War II because the best scrapers among them could not catch a dozen soft crabs in a day. Even Ed Harrison was ready to pack it in, but tough as he was, his wife was even tougher: "I'd as leave starve as move to Baltimore," she told him, and they hunkered down for the lean summer. Things came back in the '20s and the '40s. They always have, the watermen say; and God willing, they will again.

It is a deep and touching faith, born both of experience and a lack of other options in life. But the science and the statistics argue differently. They say the bay has entered a new era. The declines are too widespread and too long lasting. Natural ups and downs continue, but every decade the ups are lower, the downs deeper. And more than catches are down. The living bay bottom itself has begun to unravel. The lush meadows of underwater grasses that once spread across as much as 650,000 acres of bay bottom have died back to around a tenth of that, with no baywide comeback yet apparent. Both the grasses and oysters performed important water-quality functions that only now are being appreciated fully. Together they were able to filter and absorb and clarify from the water vast quantities of pollutants. The oysters alone, in the quantities that lay on the bay bottom a century ago, are estimated to have filtered a volume of water equal to the whole Chesapeake every few days, compared to nearly a year for today's depleted stocks. As we spend hundreds of millions of dollars on modern sewage treatment plants, we have lost natural cleansing mechanisms that did the same work for free.

Even bay species that appear to remain healthy are under severe pressure as the bay's harvesters lose more options and are forced to focus ever more intensely on what survives. Scientists, for example, do not talk so much about catches as they do about something they call "catch per unit effort." As applied to the crab, it translates like this: commercial watermen's catches have remained fairly level at around 90 million pounds in recent years; but the units of effort—i.e., crab pots—have risen in number by more than 50 percent. In short, watermen are fishing harder to maintain the same catch.

And although statistics to document it are scarce, the growth in pressure from watermen may well have been exceeded by us recreational crabbers. With our chicken necks on strings, handful of cheap crab pots, and dipnets, it never seems

like any of us are catching all that many, and we aren't. But there are 15 million people living in the Chesapeake region, and three million more moving in by the year 2020; and as of 1990, these are estimated to be catching 30 million pounds of crabs annually, not to mention other species sought for recreation.

Can we rein ourselves in on the harvests of what remains healthy? Can we bring back all that is not? Some signs point to hope. Major water-quality programs are in place across Maryland, Virginia, and Pennsylvania to control the major pollutants of the estuary. Some are working,

*(Facing and above) Brightly painted corks are used to identify the location and ownership of crab pots, baited wire-mesh traps used to catch hard crabs. During the first big runs of crabs in spring and early summer, narrow channels may be so clogged with pots that their corks impede local navigation. More than a million crab pots are estimated in use in the bay.*

others are not, and none are happening broadly and fast enough. The way, however, is clear, and the journey well begun. And there is living proof that the bay still has some capacity to cure itself if left alone. The rockfish, since near-unlimited fishing pressure was sharply curtailed in 1985, has recovered to where there may be more of that species in the bay now than at any time in modern history. It is still not certain whether the rock is reproducing well enough to be caught in more than token numbers, but the future of this quintessential Chesapeake species looks better than it has in more than a decade.

Less clear is whether fishermen and fisheries managers are ready to reject across the board the myth of unlimited abundance that has shaped harvests of the bay since the time of Captain John Smith. It might be comforting to think that if we can eliminate pollution and restore the bay to full health, we can go back to fishing without much concern about exhausting the place, and of course there is a seed of truth in that. A cleaner bay will be fantastically productive. But even a century or more ago, we showed ourselves capable of overwhelming the most pristine resources. No scientist thinks the great hauls of oysters and shad and ducks from the last century represented levels that

*Some of the bay's most dangerous fishing is winter crab dredging in Virginia, near where the Chesapeake meets the Atlantic. Here the* Loni Carol II *out of Tangier Island drags 16 feet of steel dredge in heavy winds.*

(Facing) The day this picture was taken, three crab dredgers died when their boat went down within sight of the Bay Bridge-Tunnel. Despite squalls that raked the fleet, work went on.

(Above) Balanced on the slick, heaving platform extending from the Loni Carol II's stern, Jackie McCready stuffs the semidormant crabs, a bushel at a time, into baskets. The boat caught its 75-bushel limit by lunchtime—exceptional fishing.

were sustainable. And a century later, there are not only many more of us, but technology, from bigger engines to better sonar, is making us deadly efficient fishermen. Presumably, the fish are not keeping pace.

The potential is there for a new era of responsibility in harvesting the bay, but the cold fact is that to date, we have never moved to manage any species on a sustainable basis before it crashed to historic depths. The risks of failure go well beyond economics and our eating pleasure. Many of the photographs in this book show people and cultures that are based on sustaining a healthy commercial harvest of the Chesapeake. They are on the very edge of survival, and to lose them, even as we undertake one of the nation's great environmental cleanup efforts, would be a bitter irony. Many watermen would laugh to hear themselves called "poets…who never wrote a line," but if poetry can be characterized as crystallizing feelings shared deeply by us all, then these seafood cultures, by their living close to a nature the rest of us have largely divorced, by their artistry in sieving the bay through their meshes and their lives, are indeed imparting something vital to the quality of life on the Chesapeake.

City crabber, country crabber: (facing) an urban "chicken-necker" tends his hand lines baited with poultry parts in downtown Baltimore; (above) Edward Jones, a long-time bay waterman, runs his baited trotline in Tangier Sound, dipping crabs as the line pulls them across a roller attached to his skiff.

Bobby Butler, a Chester River oysterman, harvests shellfish with hand tongs, a technique little changed from pre-Colonial times. A century ago the bottom of the Chesapeake was armored with more oysters than any place on earth. (Right and facing) Today, disease, pollution, and overfishing have left the bay with perhaps one percent of those original oyster stocks.

*Waiting on the wind, the last fleet of working sail craft in North America floats on the Choptank River at dawn on opening day of oyster dredging season. Maryland law forbids dredging oysters under power, except for Mondays and Tuesdays, when the skipjacks can use engines attached to small "push boats."*

(Facing) Perhaps half the bay's remaining working skipjacks waft here on the Choptank River, unable to rake the oyster beds with their heavy dredges until the wind comes up.

(Above) Many of the wooden skipjacks are close to a century old. Although some still carry gear like this antique compass, they also employ the latest electronics, like LORAN, which is capable of returning a boat to a good fishing spot in fog or dark.

*A crewman aboard the* Rebecca Ruark, *the oldest working skipjack, hustles to douse the jib as an unexpectedly high wind bears down on the boat.*

Begun in November's Indian summer, dredging season turns hard by February. The only heat aboard the old skipjacks comes from the tiny cook-stove in the cabin. Even worse, prices drop, and hours lengthen.

(Pages 98-99) Workdays that start long before dawn sometimes end after sunset.

Dredged by crabbers from
the near-oceanic salt waters
of the bay's mouth, knobbed
whelks provide a profitable
bonus. Their richly colored
shells are the largest in the
Chesapeake Bay.

The energetic and aggressive bluefish are migrants which spawn in the open ocean. Although the bluefish population experiences long-term cycles of abundance and scarcity, the fluctuations do not appear related to bay conditions.

(Facing) The most abundant commercial species in the bay, menhaden are used for crab bait, chicken feed, and fertilizer, and their oil is a base for cosmetics, paints, and tempering products for steel. Watermen call them "alewives" or "olwyes," which leads to confusion with their cousin, the alewife, or river herring.

(Above) The diamondback terrapin does not mature sexually for nearly a decade and may live more than 40 years. It was fished into commercial extinction during the 1930s, when prices paid by restaurants reached a dollar an inch. Less prized as food now, the terrapin has rebounded baywide.

(Facing) Kenny Heath, a Virginia fisherman out of Wise Point, stakes his nets in the waters near the mouth of the Chesapeake, an area typified by a wide range of both marine and estuarine species, including (above) horseshoe crabs, sharks, weakfish, bluefish, cownose rays, puff toads, and a barnacled sea turtle.

Purse seiners operating out of Reedville net menhaden throughout the lower Chesapeake and offshore Mid-Atlantic waters, bringing in an annual catch that averaged 400 million tons in the mid-1970s. Once fish are spotted from airplanes or the crow's-nest of the mother ship, smaller craft are lowered to encircle the school with net, which is then drawn from the bottom into a "purse."

*Once the purse seine is drawn tightly around millions of menhaden, the catch is vacuumed by huge flexible hoses into the hold of the mother ship, which then heads back to the processing plant.*

107

(Top) Throwing back the most valuable part of his catch, West River pound netter Billy Joe Groom observes the moratorium Maryland placed on rockfish in 1985 after over-fishing and reproductive failures caused their numbers to plummet. (Right) Pound netting extends a long fence of mesh out from the shore-line, intercepting whatever swims by and channeling it into the "pound," or trap portion of the net.

Carroll Lumpkin, aboard
Billy Joe Groom's boat
True Blue, *offloads the
day's haul into containers*
on deck. Only the menha-
den are kept to supply bait
to crab potters.

*"Spargas'n" is one of the more esoteric pursuits of bay watermen, who know the secret spots where wild asparagus sprouts from the salt marsh in spring.*

*(Facing) Gill netting, which entraps fish by their gill plates in the net's meshes, has largely replaced pound netting for commercial fishing. Fishing gill nets is less labor intensive than fishing the pounds. They are also more selective, as the mesh can be varied to exclude all but certain size fish. However, gill nets drown all that they catch, while unwanted or endangered species in pounds can be thrown back alive.*

(Facing) Allen Smith of Tylerton hunts a remote marsh for ducks with Luke, his constant companion.

(Above) Luke, holding a prize weakfish in his mouth, will always pick the most expensive species out of Allen's nets, his owner says.

# MIGRATIONS

Migration, the coming and going of fish and fowl, suits the Chesapeake well. The bay itself has, in a sense, been "coming" for several thousand years, since the influence of the Ice Age last waned. High seas fed by melted polar ice flooded the narrow, ancient valleys cut by the Susquehanna and James rivers, forming our present-day broad estuary. Such warming periods are brief, geologically speaking, and last for only tens of thousands of years. It will not be long, on planetary time scales, before the glaciers advance, and this bay, too, ebbs surely as the tide.

On a smaller, daily scale, coming and going is the bay's nature. Tides surge up and down the estuary, rising and falling every six hours or so like the respiration of a great sea creature. Add to this basic pattern the bay's constant coming in its deeps and going at its surface, as lighter, fresher river water slips seaward atop layers of denser, saltier ocean oozing in from the mouth.

Seasonally, a vital quality of the bay's water—its salinity—migrates up and down the estuary. In spring, high flows of river water compress the territory of salt-loving species back toward the bay's mouth in Virginia; then in autumn, weak river flow allows the ocean's influence far up into Maryland.

So it seems especially fitting that our bay, more than most places, is embroidered fantastically with nature's cycles of migration. We tend to celebrate the bay for the quantity and diversity of life that is here; yet fully as enriching are the near-constant leavings and arrivals. The passage of wild geese in autumn and the appearance of fresh soft crabs on May's restaurant menus reassure us and reset our clocks, if only briefly, to a vaster frame of reference. In an era when ecology is teaching us that everything is connected within a wide web of life, migration provides the ultimate expansion of the Chesapeake's relationships to the planet.

It was not many years ago that we began to think of the bay as a single body of water, whose natural processes recognize no political boundaries between states or counties. Even more recently, attempts to control pollution washed by rainwater from the land have expanded our focus to the watershed, the 41 million acres whose creeks and rivers all drain to the bay—an area extending

*Royal terns nesting on a remote spit of sand flare up when disturbed, their dense flight pattern creating a blizzard effect confusing to predators.*

nearly to Vermont, almost to North Carolina, and across the Alleghenies of West Virginia. Scientists are even talking of the bay's airshed, a large chunk of the eastern United States from which prevailing winds blow air pollutants that sift into the estuary, harming fish and water quality. Most extensive of all contexts for the Chesapeake, however, is the "migrationshed," the corners of the globe to which the bay annually reconnects through its farthest-traveling migrants. This stretches from Hudson Bay to the Brazilian Amazon, and from the tundra bordering the Bering Straits to the deepest abysses of the Sargasso Sea.

*Perhaps the bay's oddest amalgam of human and natural: great blue herons nest on artificial platforms erected by the U.S. Navy at its bombing range on Bloodsworth Island. Noise doesn't seem to bother the birds, which have coexisted with fighter planes and warships for years.*

The migrationshed (it begs coining a more graceful name), despite its size and tenuous integrity, is a practical concept. What happens to natural habitat half a world away may be just as vital to "our" birds and fish as controlling pollution and conserving marshes in our backyards. Conversely, we who steward the resources of the Chesapeake must realize our wider responsibility—maintenance of a link in chains of life encircling half the world. A bird or fish freshly returned to the Chesapeake from far afield brings something special with it—the message that a chain of natural ecosystems along its migration route remains intact and clean enough to perpetuate its annual cycle.

The author and naturalist Barry Lopez, writing of migration in the far north, observes: "Watching the animals come and go, and feeling the land swell up to meet them and then feeling it grow still at their departure, I came to think of the migrations as breath, as the land breathing. In spring a great inhalation of light and animals. The long-bated breath of summer. And an exhalation that propelled them all south in the fall." Migration in the Chesapeake country is less compressed than the short-summered Arctic's, of course; nor are some of the most important migrations here necessarily long or spectacular. There is scarcely a month or a week on the bay when something is not moving in or out, or preparing to do so. Following is a short calendar of Chesapeake migration, by no means inclusive.

February, and the great blue herons come early to nest, bringing welcome reassurance of spring well before most other fish or fowl. Once on a February 6th, I was hiking a bay marsh on one of the nastiest, windiest, sleetiest days I can recall. The winter had been hard, and looked as if it had

*The great blue heron's family evolved more than 60 million years ago and has not changed a great deal since—one of nature's more successful experiments.*

staying power. Then overhead, I heard a guttural croaking. A pair of great blues circled on the storm, heading for a clump of tall trees where last summer's nests were piled high with snow and ice. What powerful urges must lure them from the balmier Carolinas and Florida at such times, certain even as winter grips hardest that warmth and food aplenty will soon emerge to ensure the survival of another generation of Chesapeake-born chicks.

March, and by St. Patrick's Day, the ospreys have begun to show. Like the herons, they do not come and go in the spectacular masses of the waterfowl; but they are nonetheless great travelers. These large fish hawks, whose nests crown thousands of bay channel markers and buoys, commonly live for 15 years, and in that time the osprey may travel more than 100,000 miles. Eastern Brazil is the commonest wintering destination for Chesapeake ospreys, but some go as far south as Uruguay and Chile.

April, and the rivers start filling with traffic. Most of the anadromous fishes—those that run from the sea up rivers to spawn—are schooling in the river mouths. White perch, yellow perch, hickory, and American shad are all pushing to get on with it; but my personal pick is the common river herring, *Alosa pseudoharengus*, a silver, 10 to

12-inch specimen, too bony for anything but pickling, that thrashes its way to the utter ends of the bay's tributaries. Before dams were built to block them, the little alosa used to reach up the James watershed past Charlottesville and into the mountain foothills. Up the Susquehanna, they traversed all of Pennsylvania and into New York to lay their eggs. I can't think of a better place to be in April than camped beside a herring stream when squadrons of alosa begin finning across the sun-spangled sand and gravel shallows, frothing the deeper water of dark bends. Thousands of miles of creek that appear relatively barren for 48 weeks of the year are suddenly glutted with writhing, silvered life.

It represents the end of a journey that began with the herring somehow homing from hundreds of miles out to sea onto the precise little stream where they were born. No one has fully explained it; but it means that each waterway makes a singular reconnection with the seas and with whatever mysterious and elemental mechanisms are employed to maintain the annual traffic between the two.

May is busy, busy, busy; but I'll pick the rockfish anytime as May's migrant. A rockfish can weigh more than 75 pounds and attain lengths of several feet. They are, except for the rare stray shark, the biggest seagoer that journeys up the bay's tributaries. It is an awesome experience to be afloat in a canoe on a quiet, dark reach of a river and hear the silence of a May evening shattered by the rolling of a huge cow striper, attended by a dozen smaller, leaping males. Once spring nights on the bay echoed to the crash of an even mightier river spawner, which reached lengths of more than

*(Facing) The heron's young grasp the bill of an adult returning to the nest, triggering a regurgitation reflex. The chicks ravenously consume half-digested crabs and fish as they issue from the parent's long beak.*

*(Above) These great blue heron chicks are all legs and beaks, a few weeks away from flying and feeding on their own. Herons thrive in every county of the Chesapeake's six-state drainage basin.*

10 feet and weighed more than 500 pounds; but the Atlantic sturgeon was virtually exterminated by pollution and overfishing by the 1930s.

In fact, most of the species of fish in serious decline around the bay seem to be its anadromous types. Perhaps it is partly that the upriver portions of the estuary they depend on for spawning and nurseries are closer to and more vulnerable to sources of human pollution. Additionally, the migratory habits of the anadromous fish—funneling at predictable times into narrow waterways in great numbers—have made them supremely vulnerable to overfishing. In many bay rivers and streams, rockfish, shad, and herring were greeted with nets that virtually cordoned off the entire path to the spawning grounds. Currently, the worst of the fishing excesses have been stopped: the rock is recovering nicely, the herring are hanging in there at much-reduced levels, and the shad may, just may, be mounting a painfully slow comeback. There is even an experimental effort to release baby sturgeon into the wild from hatcheries.

Summer, and throughout the months of June,

*Bald eagle chicks survey the bay from 70 feet up in a loblolly pine. (Facing) An osprey, or fish hawk, sentinels the salt marsh from its nest atop an abandoned crab trap in Tangier Sound. Both species have made comebacks since the banning of DDT, which weakened their eggshells and caused high mortality in unhatched chicks.*

(Above) Probably the most ubiquitous bird in the bay region, the herring gull thrives in Baltimore Harbor, and (facing) nests successfully on piles of dredged spoils overgrown with phragmites reeds.

July, and August, some of the bay's most important migrations take place in a few days or hours. Summertime seems reserved for the short-trippers, whose mininavigational feats are no less remarkable for not involving great distances.

Diamondback terrapins, a species spread throughout the Chesapeake and its rivers, appear to live and die within a small radius of where they were born. Maybe it is one reason they live so long—more than 40 years in many cases. They are secretive souls, seldom showing more than a black head poked briefly above the surface to reconnoiter. Once on Smith Island I was swimming off a remote bay beach when I noticed a long line of terrapin heads moving purposefully southward down the bay, following the shoreline. It was the first time I had ever seen such a group movement, and the line passed with only minor breaks for nearly half an hour. I never knew where they were headed, but in light of recent research, they were likely females homing in on a very specific and close-by nesting beach. If a terrapin's "home" patch of beach has been developed or altered by human presence, it appears that it simply won't come ashore to reproduce. Even when the coast looks clear, nesting terrapins take no chances. Scientists have spent interminable hours hunkered down

Springtime is ushered in at Jimmys Creek on the Nanticoke River and thousands of other bay tributaries by the spawning surges of alewives and blueback herrings, which home in from the Atlantic Ocean to the same waters where they were born.

in blinds, watching female diamondbacks bob in the water just off their chosen beach, watching, checking for any sign of disturbance before emerging to lay as many as 20 leathery-soft eggs in the warm sand. The slightest movement or irregularity ashore—the barking of a dog—can send them back offshore for hours. Though terrapins nest baywide each summer by the thousands, few people have ever witnessed their annual ritual, and few ever will.

The bay, we said earlier, has a two-layered flow, fresher water always moving seaward near the surface and saltier water always pushing up-bay near the bottom. The tides may reverse this at times, but the net movement is always the same. Several creatures who must migrate while they are still far too feeble to move on their own hitch rides on this north-south express simply by moving vertically a short distance. Rise in the water, and you catch the southbound (fresh, flowing toward Norfolk); sink, and you're on the northbound (salt, headed for Baltimore). A key rider of the bay express is the larval Chesapeake oyster, making the only migration of its life. After being spawned during June through August, the oyster is a microscopic, free-floating larva. It has two to three weeks to find a suitable place on the bay

*The diamondback terrapin also appears to home in on the same stretches of beach to bury its eggs each year. Here a just-hatched terrapin makes its way to the safety of the water.*

bottom to attach and form a permanent home. If it fails, it dies. The oyster larva, it turns out, has an exquisite sensitivity to variations in salinity. It is able to differentiate between fresher and saltier water, and by sinking or rising it can move upstream, downstream, or, by alternately sinking and rising, simply hold a stable position in its search for a good home. This migration need not be far. Salinity can double in the bay's layered flows in a vertical distance of only eight inches.

But a trip of a foot or two is just as critical to survival of the bay's oysters as any global odyssey of the osprey.

September, October, and November, and the great spectacles begin to fill the air. Waterfowl from across the hemisphere's northern latitudes begin to flow, first in streams, then joining as rivers, converging more than a million strong on the marshes and waters of the bay by late autumn. From eastern Canada's remote Ungava Peninsula come the Canada geese; redheads, canvasbacks, widgeon, pintail, and dozens of other species arrive from prairie potholes and river deltas across Alberta, Manitoba, and Saskatchewan. Last in, but perhaps most spectacular of all, are the tundra swans which nest across Alaska's North Slope and into Siberia. These giants, with wingspreads nearly seven feet, stage in late November near the Canada-U.S. border in North Dakota. There they wait to catch the coattails of a blustery cold front, riding it south to the bay in one incredible nonstop flight that may be up to 1,200 miles long.

Amid all these autumnal comings there is a massive departure that scarcely ever gets noticed, though it occurs throughout virtually every thread of water across the six-state watershed.

Usually moving at night, on the dark of the moon, eels begin coursing down every stream of the bay drainage. They are the bay's only true catadromous species, running downriver to the ocean to spawn. Along with eels from all over North America, Europe, and the Mediterranean, they are drawn by forces we know nothing of toward a single destination, a supersaline, stagnant region of the Atlantic known as the Sargasso Sea. Here, after swimming thousands of miles without eating, their bodies badly deteriorated except for reproductive organs, half a world of eels mix their sperm and eggs and sink slowly into the cold depths to die.

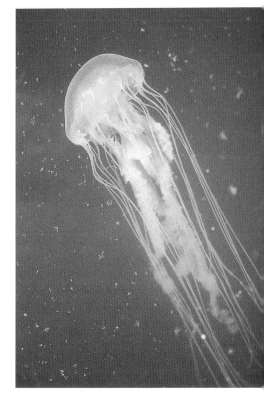

Months and even years later, great, slow oceanic currents will deliver some of the billions of baby eels thus produced to the mouth of the Chesapeake. From there they will navigate into every corner of the watershed, surmounting dams that halt other species, pressing as far as West Virginia and Pennsylvania. Then they will settle down to a residence that can last well over a decade before they hear the Sargasso's call in their genes, and begin their long journey.

December and January, and migration winds down, nearing low ebb. In the deep channels,

*(Facing) A brown pelican, another comeback story since the banning of DDT, prepares to swallow lunch filched from a fisherman's pound net.*

*(Above) No body of water on earth produces stinging nettles with the regularity and abundance of the Chesapeake.*

sooks are still scuttling toward Virginia to bury themselves for the winter, beautifully done up for autumn with their blue and ivory claws tipped a vivid, fiery red; but soon, even the sooks stop moving. Perhaps for a few weeks the bay is absolutely without migration. But even in coldest January the days have begun to lengthen. Far out to sea the longer days have triggered the herring to begin moving coastward. On Georgia bayous a few great blue herons must be fidgeting and facing north more frequently. And somewhere between Bermuda and Cape Charles, larval eels revolve lazily in the grip of a current pushing them bayward. In the vast migrationshed of the Chesapeake, something is always coming or going.

*Tundra swans haul their 20-pound bodies in nonstop flights of more than a thousand miles on their annual migration to the bay from as far away as Alaska's North Slope. Distinctive patterns of yellow on a black beak (below) distinguish tundras from mute swans.*

*(Pages 130-131) Canada geese have adapted better than any other of the bay's waterfowl species to the decline of the submerged aquatic vegetation that once was their main food. They now feed in grain fields.*

*It may be up to young Julia Teal Baugh and her contemporaries to restore the bay's vitality, so that creatures like the river herring her father caught on its journey from open ocean to bay creek will continue to enthrall future generations.*

My introduction to life along the Chesapeake came in the mid 1950s, when my father would pack my older brother Joe and me into the Chevy, throw in the 2HP Evenrude, and head for Williamsport, Maryland, at the confluence of the Conococheague Creek and the Potomac River. We'd fish for sunnies and bass, swim, and explore Duck Island not far upstream. I will forever be grateful to my father for those experiences.

In those days, I didn't think about where the water that flowed under our boat went, but I have since, and Tom Horton is largely responsible. I can't think of anyone with whom I'd rather run aground.

Numerous watermen showed me the Chesapeake as their families have known it for generations: Bobby Butler, Billy Joe Groom, Kenny Heath, Edward, Daniel, and Mike Harrison; Edward Jones, Ralph Lee, Dwight Marshall, Wadey Murphy, "Bunks" Mitchell, Lonnie Moore, and Alan Smith. The staffers at the Chesapeake Bay Foundation also pointed me in the right direction: Don Baugh, Denny Bradshaw, Rod Coggin, Chuck Foster, Bill Goldsborough, Sandy Hillyer, Steve Fletcher, Don Jackson, Caroline Kurrus, Brendan Sweeney, Ted Wilgis, and a host of CBF educators.

Some of the photographs in this book were made while Tom and I were on assignment for CBF; thanks to Will Baker, Elizabeth Buckman, and Mary Todd Winchester for their guidance on that project. The Anne Arundel County Commission on Culture and the Arts, Baltimore Sun, Chesapeake Bay Trust, National Geographic Society, National Fish and Wildlife Foundation, Times Mirror Foundation, and Virginia Foundation for the Humanites and Public Policy were generous in their support.

Finally, I'd like to thank my wife Barbara and daughters Hilary and Alison for their unflagging encouragement and for tolerating my many absences from home while working on *Water's Way*.

David W. Harp
Baltimore